The Pursuit
of
Passion

Thoughts to Help You Navigate
From the Darkest Hours to
the Light of Inspiration

by George Kahn

ISBN-13: 9781492827054 Photo, illustration, and text credits constitute an extension of this
copyright page.

PRAISE FOR THE PURSUIT OF PASSION

"I don't get up early enough for the sunrise, but reading George's posts of the Passion Party are the next best thing. A very inspirational and thought-provoking way to start the day. Kind of a creative kick-in-the-ass." **Mark Zaslove, television and magazine writer**

"Usually we're running flat-out just to keep up. George reminds us to catch our breath and consider what's really important: Why am I doing this? Where am I going?" **Roger Gillott, Crisis PR guru, President, Gillott Communications**

"George's Passion Party writings have inspired me to be a better person and to realize what is truly important in life." **Eric Epstein, attorney**

"Through his thoughts and insights shared in this marvelous collection, George shines a light on my soul and raises my awareness that all is possible if I care, share and listen, to know when to lead, when to follow and when to let go and let God." **Craig Lamar, realtor**

"George's ruminations, though they vary as to topic, almost always hearken back to basic themes of service, integrity, and enthusiasm—all basic keys to success in any endeavor. He jangles those keys for us, lest they have sat too long in our pocket without our having acted upon them." **Mark Gershenson, attorney**

"Like a jazz improviser for whom encyclopedic knowledge of the scales and the canon is a mere jumping off point, George has managed to synthesize an enormous amount of familiar self-improvement strategy and thought into something very original, personal, and, dare I say, of spiritual value to the reader." **Brian Diedrich, Digital Advertising Executive**

"Each day I take a minute vacation from work, take a deep breath, and I read the latest Passion Party blog. Then I return to my work, feeling refreshed and a bit more creative." **Jim Wilberger, Film Director, The Hallmark Channel**

"The Passion Party always seems to be just the exact message I needed to hear. It holds me accountable each day to read, think, evaluate, and implement." **Kathie Moore, CRS, realtor**

"I work in the always connected world of electronic devices, and George's passion party is refreshing. His posts often show the importance of making time for a face to face conversation, and giving all my attention to the people around me." **Asher Dahan, Accurate Data Networks, Inc.**

"What's really important: self-honesty, kindness, humor, love, and staying focused – the Passion Party writings are such great reminders." **Mary K., paralegal**

" I have been keeping George's 'musings' in a separate folder on my computer. I keep them because they are just too thought-provoking, touching, funny, true, insightful and/or clever to delete.   I always look forward to the next one… **Debbi Kanoff, retired lawyer**

"George's Passion Party blog brightens my life, gives me a smile, and presents a real perspective on what's important in today's convoluted world." **Chris Lebenzon, film producer and editor**

"I receive hundreds of emails every day. I save "The Passion Party" for that part of the day when I want to take a holiday from the prosaic to think beyond my current reach. It is my midday vacation---and inspiration." **Michael B. Altman, CLU, ChFC, Altman & Kabaker**

"When I open my e-mail and find the most recent posting to Passion Party from George, it always makes me smile. It's funny how someone else's take on the issues we all grapple with every day can unexpectedly open a door into our own thinking and bring light where none may have existed before. George's pure take on these weighty matters of heart and soul gives me the comfort to know I'm not struggling alone." **Janet Duffy, freelance writer, *"Easy As Writing"***

"I find George's blog very insightful and refreshing, filled with info that pertains to journey in this thing we call life." **M.B. Gordy..... Los Angeles-based freelance musician and composer**

"When a person integrates the practical and the artistic, the material and the spiritual, I listen. The world has more than enough disconnection; I am inspired by people who put things together. Real passion flows from these poems, the product of a mind and heart in synch." **Rabbi Shmuel Klatzkin**

For my mom,

Marcia Kahn,

who taught me to always create,

no matter what.

TABLE OF CONTENTS

Introduction IX

Foreward XI

Change Or Die 1

Whatever It Takes 3

A Stream Of Abundance 5

Restart My Heart 6

What Can I Give You Today? 8

Environment 10

I Love Who I Am Becoming 12

It's Not Easy 14

Confidence Box 16

Play Big 18

Don't Hold Back 20

Do It Anyway 22

The Importance Of Being Passionate 23

Time for Passion 25

Time To Risk 27

Sleepers, Awake! 28

Big Dreams 29

Dance Like No One Is Watching 31

The Pursuit of Passion 33

My Purpose 35

Unbury The Passion 36

Thin, Rich and Happy 37

The Why 39

Finding The Core 41

10,000 Hours 43

Early To Rise 45

50 Years Plus 1 (Reflections On The End Of A Decade) ...47

Self-Esteem 49

Purposeful Action 51

Up Your Game 52

Accountability 54

Inspect What You Expect 56

Life Purpose Mad Libs 58

What Do You Love? 61

The Mountain 62

Attack Life With Enthusiasm 64

The Week That Will Be 66

The Dance Of Life 67

The Muse In Music 69

A Dream 71

Give What You Can —With Passion 72

Creativity 73

Momentum 74

Walk Through Fire 75

Competence — Excellence — Brilliance 77

Love The Process 79

Launching Pad 81

Life Is Short 83

The Best Thing 84

Fear of Flying 85

Fear of Flying (part 2) 87

What If It Works? 89

Actualizing Inspiration Formula 91

Full-Heartedness 92

Honing Your Vision 93

Be More Human 94

The Power Of Gratitude 96

Passion and Skill 98

Inspiration Is Overrated 99

A Sense of Adventure..100

Obstacles 101

Anniversary 102

My Wish 103

Acknowledgments 105

About the Artwork 107

About the Author 109

INTRODUCTION

These writings came from a promise. Right before Memorial Day 2009, I met with my business coach Joe Stumpf. After 20 years as a commissioned loan officer, I had just lived through possibly the worst year ever in the business. My previous company had collapsed in the mortgage meltdown of 2008. During the previous 12 months my assistant had earned more money than I had. About 50% of the people in my industry were either out of work or actively looking for jobs in other areas of business. Things looked bleak, and there was no fun left. Work had become a painful grind with very little financial reward to show for all the time spent.

I shared my total burnout in the business of 20 years with my coach. Frustrated by what my life had become, it became clear that something had to give. Either I had to change jobs, or change my attitude. Maybe both! I promised to get up at 5:00 AM every day to meditate and journal, to focus on bringing passion back into every aspect of my life, my work, my family, and my personal growth. Instead of going to work every day and having a pity party, I have decided to have a passion party.

These writings (a sample of the 475+ entries from the website http://passionparty09.blogspot.com) are the outgrowth of that commitment. I hope they inspire you to find your passion, and that you enjoy reading them as much as I did writing them.

George Kahn

November 2012

THE NEW AMERICAN DREAM

Be remarkable
Be generous
Create art
Make judgment calls
Connect people and ideas
...and we have no choice but to reward you.

–Seth Godin (from "Linchpin")

CHANGE OR DIE

It began out of frustration.
My life was stuck in a downward spiral of
hard work, dislikes, and have-to's. I had lost my passion for
the business.

The question was, "What one thing can you change today to
raise your frequency, to help pull yourself and other people
up?"

I thought for a moment and said,
"I guess I could meditate. I used to meditate. But my life is
so busy, my business feels so out of control, I don't have the
time."

"What if you got up at 5:00 AM to meditate?"
I thought about it. There is no way I could wake up at 5:00
AM every day. Don't even ask me.

"What if you commit to meditation for 21 days?
One day at a time, for 21 days, you get up at 5:00 AM,
meditate, and then write your inspirational thought for the
day."

"I guess I could do that. For 21 days."

"Good. Then pick a dozen or so friends, and every morning
after you write in your journal, send them the post."

I saw what was happening.

Action
Commitment
Accountability

So I agreed to reinvent myself every morning, to get in touch with my passion, for 21 days.
And so I joined the 5:00 AM Club, and the passion party was born.

WHATEVER IT TAKES

About 33 years ago I let go of my possessions, threw a few things into a Dodge van, and moved to Los Angeles. I decided to do whatever it takes to start a new life as a musician and composer. I would be a pianist/composer in Hollywood, a musical "gunslinger" for hire.

About 23 years ago, when my son was two years old, I got my first job in finance. It had been ten years of grabbing scraps from Hollywood's musical buffet table, and it was time to move on. "Road work" was not an option; the hit song remained illusory. I looked at my watch and it said, "Time to get a real job."

I had decided to do whatever it takes to shift into a new career. A crash course in the Series 7 license got me a job at a municipal bond firm, which got me a job as a stockbroker in the Roaring '80s.

Three years later I knew I was not meant to be a stockbroker, and I moved into banking.

About 20 years ago I got my first job as a loan officer for Columbia Savings and Loan. I decided to do whatever it takes to be a successful loan officer. I rapidly learned that this meant leaving behind a regular paycheck and becoming a commission-based "salesperson".

About 11 years ago I was burnt out after the real estate crash in the '90s, and was ready to try something new. I decided to do whatever it takes to build a mortgage business built on trust and honesty that would allow me to earn a great income and still have time for my music, my family and my life.

It is now 2009. After a long ride of financial success, my mortgage business collapsed with the rest of the economy. Life is a struggle. Any fun that existed in my business has been sucked out.

I am here now. Once again, I am ready to do whatever it takes to rekindle the passion in my life.

A STREAM OF ABUNDANCE

It is so easy to get pulled down right now. News is bleak. The media drum beat has been negative for years. Recession — layoffs — budget deficits.

Half the people that were in my part of the banking industry are out of work or selling phones. When I tell people at a party I am a mortgage banker they move to the other side of the room.

But still, the sun rises every morning on another day filled with potential and opportunity. My life is filled with people I love, a caring wife and two great kids. The birds gather to eat and sing at the feeder outside my window. Like them, I have a chance to make music on any given day.

Life is beautiful if I stop for a moment and just observe it. Nature continues its steady pace from spring to summer. I do not have to make summer arrive. It just does.

All I need to do today is take a ride on the stream of abundance.

Let the passion party begin!

RESTART MY HEART

My battery died yesterday.

No, really.

I went down to the parking garage and the car would not start.
I had to call AAA.

The car is less than three years old; this should not be
happening. I shook my fist and cursed the car industry for
designing a car that turns its own lights off and yet is given a
weak battery that goes dead all by itself.

It took about 20 minutes for the man to show up and I ended
picking up my son Evan late from school. It was an annoyance
and inconvenience for both of us.

I have been paying my AAA membership dutifully for many
years. I was happy to call them again today to help me. I
was so thrilled that I just have to call this 800 number, and
someone will ride to the rescue and get my battery started.

But who will I call to restart my heart?

My heart yearns for joy and passion and yet it often feels
clogged with the day-to-day demands of life.

Sometimes I have to bring it to the repair shop: it could be the ocean, or a dirt road in the country, where I allow my brain, my heart, my body and soul to reconnect and check in with each other.

I wish I could have a man come with a little energy box, hook up the cables and — BAM! — I'm up and running again.

Maybe I can. I just have to find the man with the little box of energy. I have his number here somewhere...

WHAT CAN I GIVE YOU TODAY?

Diana, my wife, broke her foot two weeks ago. We like to say she did it kickboxing, but actually she tripped in a dark concert hall.

She is two weeks into the cast and the crutches and the physical therapy, and I am two weeks into being her caretaker. It is a relatively small thing in the world of problems, but it adds a layer of complexity to everyday life as I am picking up a lot of the extra jobs around the house that Diana usually handles.

I am not great at wrangling a vacuum cleaner. And who knew there could be so many dirty dishes?

At first it felt like yet another thing to take care of. And then I realized, I don't want to be her caretaker — I want to be her caregiver.

When I give care it is easy and open. It is the same with my clients and the people I work with.

I have so much to give.

When I clean the house for Diana my heart feels light.

When I make a pot of coffee the other person feels better, and that makes me feel better.

This is why I love giving little things, like chocolate chip cookies for almost no reason.

Giving with passion feels best of all.

I can do this today:

Find my passion, and give it away!

ENVIRONMENT

Nothing can cool passion faster

than a lousy environment.

The musician needs the right environment for the muse to visit;

the lover needs the right environment for trust and lust to join together.

I took five days off the other week to visit family,

and in the end I felt fearful.

The fear was that I had lost my center,

afraid of returning to my job

afraid of the economy

afraid of disappointing people

afraid business will dry up, that the music gigs will stop, that my family will stop loving me—afraid of illness and death.

It all felt hard, scary and uncontrollable.

Someone once said, "A family vacation is an oxymoron."

But yesterday I awoke to a loving wife

who let me cry on her shoulder

a long-needed cry.

And when I got to work, I found

the fear was just

false expectations appearing real.

My office was still there

my systems still in place

business was humming, and I was able to just drop in,
regroup, and hum along.

I felt my

passion rise again:

the passion to see what I can do to make life better for others.

I LOVE WHO I AM BECOMING

I love who I am becoming, wild and improper

I rebel in excess.

I stayed up too late last night, maybe to prove I still can

Yes, I can still be the guy at the Billy Idol concert yelling "More, More, More!"

What is that about?

It's not about being my highest, best self

the burn in my stomach today is not from passion but from yesterday's excess.

I am only human.

I am imperfect.

I never promised to be anything else.

And still there is a spark of a higher calling, no matter how hard I try to bury it.

I love who I am becoming

getting up, showing up every morning.

IT'S NOT EASY

I used to have an affirmation, "Money comes to me, easily and effortlessly."

Right now that affirmation does not ring true. Things are not easy now. Work takes a lot of effort.

Money is tight. It is a struggle to get things done.

Regulation and bureaucracy has increased and the banks are afraid to lend.

Is this true? Maybe. But this statement seems truer:

Money is flowing. It is a challenge to get things done.

I love challenges.

I love puzzles, and I love competition.

Competition allows me to win by comparison, because I am better than 90% of the people in my profession. Each person's financial ability and financial needs are a puzzle waiting to be solved.

And the business is not easy.

I always remember: if it were easy, everyone would do it.

If it were easy and effortless getting a home mortgage, I would be out of a job.

If it were easy and effortless to have a fulfilling, meaningful life, everyone would have one.

A meaningful life,

a life of passion,

takes skill, courage, knowledge and discipline.

And that is a wonderful thing.

CONFIDENCE BOX

There are days when I get so beat up

I begin to doubt myself

my knowledge turns to dust

I get defensive, angry and ready to quit.

I feel like a faker, a fraud

I lose any sense of self-worth.

At times like this I need my Confidence Box.

Hidden in the back of a drawer is an old cigar box

filled with mementos:

my back-stage pass from when I was a touring rock 'n' roll
musician

the gold ring my dad gave me

a picture of the Dodge Van that brought me to California

a picture of my wife and kids

my largest paycheck

a photo of me playing music with world-class musicians

a list of upcoming vacations for the year

the photo of me hiking the Inca Trail in Peru, fit and healthy

small photos of my mentors and heroes (Charles Ives,
Lincoln, Edison, Leonard Bernstein...)

thank you notes from home buyers that I have helped

a list of the 10 things I most want to do before I die

And suddenly, life does not seem so bad

this too shall pass,

my worth confirmed.

PLAY BIG

And as we let our light shine, we unconsciously give other people permission to do the same.
—*Marianne Williamson*

Bigger is not always better.

Sometimes bigger is just bigger.

Look at GM. Look at AIG.

Look at Six Flags — this company grew to be the biggest operator of amusement parks in the US by purchasing other parks. They declared bankruptcy a little while ago.

There is a difference between getting big and playing big.

You can buy things to get big–

playing big is an internal game.

You can consume things to get big–

playing big is a state of mind.

You can acquire things to get big–

playing big builds on your unique ability.

Today I choose to play big. I was not put on this Earth to play small.

Playing small does not serve me or others. I can shine my light, turn on my high beams. I have so much to give, and nothing to lose!

I love to play big, surrounding myself with people that help elevate me to the next level.

When I recorded my first jazz album I could have called up friends and recorded in a garage. Instead I called the best studio cats in Los Angeles to play with me in a Hollywood recording studio.

And if I can't play big here, it must be time to find a better playground!

DON'T HOLD BACK

How much of my time is spent in the realm of the mind?

And how much more powerful would it be if I connected it with my heart?

There is something deep that happens when I feel connected from my head to my toes. I can feel life coursing through my body and almost anything is possible.

My mind, like a racehorse,

Needs my heart to lead it.

My body, like a cart,

Can travel swifter and surer when heart and mind are aligned.

I spend so much time holding back,

being "careful", not wanting to rock the boat, staying in my comfort zone.

How much more could get done, how much more would be accomplished

if I would play full out all the time?

What do I have to lose?

Don't hold back!

It does not serve you.

Today I will live in my heart

I will live in passion

I will love until my heart overflows.

Don't hold back!

It does not protect you.

It gets in the way of your greatness.

If you lead with your heart,

the brain will catch up in time.

DO IT ANYWAY

Where is your passion today?

Where is your desire?

Where can it lead you?

To a field of diamonds, to a place of helping, not hurting,

To a place of sharing my highest self.

Where is my passion today?

Where is my desire?

What can I do today to feed that passion?

So often the actions I take today create results three or six months in the future.

What action can I take today that will make my future brighter, more passionate six months from now?

Listen to the voices that say, "You can't do that because…"

Tell them, "Thank you for sharing,"

and then do it anyway!

THE IMPORTANCE OF BEING PASSIONATE

I first started keeping a journal as a freshman in college. It was one of those seminal classes — Philosophy 101 — my professor was Peter Diamondopolous. Our first assignment was to keep a daily journal of our thoughts.

He said, "A life worth journaling is a life worth living."

We read Camus, Sartre and Dostoyevsky. I learned a lot.

It was somewhere during those four years of college that I realized how important passion is to me.

Not just the passion of love, but the passion of life.

I became a music major in my sophomore year. At the time I said I did it because I couldn't think of what else would keep me interested in school for three more years. Now looking back, it was the one thing I felt most passionate about.

Passion is the difference between running away and running towards.

It is the fuel of desire.

You can have a burning desire for something, but if you're not passionate about it, it's likely to fall by the wayside.

Now, all these years later, it feels good to tap that passion again.

TIME FOR PASSION

What are you passionate about?

What leaps to mind first?

Now, have you spent any time on your passion in the last week?

For some people their job is their life.

Other people have already created a life

where their job is their passion

I want a life

where my passion is my job.

Some people are more multifaceted,

the job is a tool that helps them get to their passion

others feel trapped in a job,

just trying to make ends meet.

For me, my job creates the financial freedom to allow me to pursue my passion:

the bliss of playing music with others in a creative setting

the amazing experience of sitting down with a blank piece of manuscript paper and pencil, and having a musical composition appear fully formed.

This is the week I say

Time to stop

and create time for my passion.

TIME TO RISK

"And the day came when the risk it took to remain tight in the bud was more painful than the risk it took to blossom." —Anais Nin

Summer is here

the days are long

It is time to risk

the one thing you have thought about doing

but were afraid to try.

SLEEPERS, AWAKE!

---

*"There is only one time when it is essential to awaken.
That time is now"* —Buddha

Some times it is hard to get up

the night time seduces me with it's quiet.

I don't want to reach full consciousness yet,

and the morning in bed is so comforting.

The June gloom does not help

casting a gray lull over the morning.

It makes things damp and

feels more like autumn than

the full blaze of summer.

I woke up today, not looking for redemption, but for
enlightenment.

Now is the time—

the roses know it, as do the pole beans and tomatoes—

that the days are too long to waste.

BIG DREAMS

I love big dreams–

Traveling around the world

Visiting exotic places

Running my own company

Performing at concert halls in major cities

Having more money than I can ever spend in a lifetime

I hate big dreams–

They are an illusion, a distraction.

They only lead to disappointment

They don't get fulfilled and

I am left with a sense of failure.

But if I don't dream big

I will never know my limits

I will not know which way to turn

I will not be able to see progress.

If I have big dreams

I can take steps towards them

And if it is really about the journey and not the destination

Then there will be no regrets

As I am on the right path.

DANCE LIKE NO ONE IS WATCHING

There is a 100-year old philosophical riddle,

"If a tree falls in the forest and no one is around to hear it, does it make a sound?" The answer seems to be that the sound is attached to the observation of the action.

We went out last night and saw a belly-dancing show.

A group of lovely ladies, all ages and sizes,

displaying traditional and fusion dances filled with isolation of movement.

This is a wonder of creation

that whether we had shown up last night or not

the dance would have gone on

the costumes would have been worn

the music would have played

and the dancers would dance.

The dance goes on.

You don't need an audience

you just need the spirit and desire

to enter the dance.

It has already begun:

I can dance today

like no one is watching.

THE PURSUIT OF PASSION

I would rather be in the pursuit of passion

than in the pursuit of happiness.

Somewhere during my childhood passion became one of the emotions I realized was a key.

From a very early age I was interested in creating things. When I was ten my friend Joe and I would rather make our own board game than play Chutes and Ladders.

Later this creative passion led me to writing newspaper articles, having a radio show, acting, photographing, film making, and in the end, having a lifelong passion for music composition and theory.

This was a love affair that was deep and mysterious. And like any great love affair, the more I gave, the more I got.

The less I felt in competition with others, the more my creative passion blossomed.

So I made a decision:

I would avoid jealousy and hatred

I would pursue passion and joy and love.

I have felt jealousy, and it's a gnawing, destructive emotion.

It pulls you and those around you down. It comes from a sense of lack, from not having enough.

I have felt passion, and it is a powerful emotion:

Talent + experience + passion = unstoppable

Passion is the fuel that keeps the fire burning.

MY PURPOSE

Passion is the fuel that keeps the fire burning

When attached to my purpose in life.

What is my purpose?

I know I was not put here on earth solely to procreate or make money.

What is the reason I am here?

The voice inside tells me, "To leave the world a better place than when I arrived."

And how best to do that?

Serve others

Share my talents

Love those around me

Be an inspiration.

UNBURY THE PASSION

Very often my passion gets buried in the process.

Every day the world sets up more rules to follow,

more road blocks.

I think of the idea I am most passionate about.

Then I think of the process to get there,

the list of actions and activities to make

this dream into a reality.

The list gets longer and more detailed

and in the end I begin to think — is it worth it?

The passionate idea has been beaten down

by the process of getting there.

The challenge is to keep the passion through the process.

To dig deep down and find the passion every day,

find the part that you love, that brought you here in the first place,

and just do that today.

THIN, RICH AND HAPPY

I read a small article yesterday.

It was a list of the ten things to do to get to your goals.

It was very seductive.

I remember a time when that was all I needed,

a list of five or ten things to do,

and "Just Do It" was my motto.

It looks so simple on paper

but there is a deeper, more important game to play.

It is not the *what you do*

and it is not the *how you do it.*

There are websites now where you can find

how to do most anything, from how to fold a shirt to how to

fly a fighter jet.

If the "how" were all you needed, everyone would be thin,
rich and happy.

The "what to do" is easy,

the "how to do" is easy,

it is the "why" that matters–

why am I doing this? Why is it important to me?

This is the drive behind the drive,

where passion lies waiting

to be awoken.

If you have a strong enough why

you can always find the how.

THE WHY

"All men should strive to learn before they die what they are running from, and to, and why." –JAMES THURBER

The "how" is easy.

The how you can watch on YouTube

or various other places on the internet

You can buy a book on "how" at Home Depot.

The how is uniform

the "why" is personal.

The why helps me grow and evolve:

especially if I plunge to the deeper questions.

Once you get beyond, "my dad was too busy to love me" or "my mom smothered me" or whatever your believe your story is...

Once you get unstuck from the story that others made for you,

you can start realizing that

you — you — made choices to run from some things, and towards others...

And then, you can discover "why?"

The why is hard, but profound, and worthy of the search.

FINDING THE CORE

I keep asking myself the question,
"What do you really want to do?"

Once I get past the ego
of how great I am
or how talented
or what a great composer
or I am writing a symphony,
the world deserves to hear my brilliance,
blah blah blah

Once I get all that out of the way
what is left?
I want to help people
I want to be of service
not just to the greater good
but to specific people,

to see the improvements and results.

Perhaps it is to help someone who never thought they could buy a property to get their first home,

or help someone living with mountains of debt to see that it is possible to climb out of that hole, one step at a time,

or lift someone's spirits when they are trapped in a snow-bound tent in the Yosemite back-country with only food, water and an iPod with my music on it,

or to be the best dad I can be for my sons by giving them time when that was all I had to give.

This is the core of my passion.

10,000 HOURS

It takes time to get really good

at anything.

Hours and hours of practice and focus

of repetitive activity and training.

Whether it's to be a construction estimator

or a doctor

or a tennis pro

or a professional musician.

And even then, in this world of overabundance,

there is no guarantee that what you have trained for

will be the career you will make your living at.

So you must love the journey.

The book "Outliers" by Malcolm Gladwell

states that it takes 10,000 hours to reach that level of excellence.

Behind every "overnight success" is 10,000 hours of training.

10,000 hours

= 1,000 hours for ten years

= three hours a day of practice

333 days a year, for ten years.

Love the journey.

EARLY TO RISE

"No one who can rise before dawn 360 days fails to make his family rich." —Ancient Chinese Proverb

There is wonder

in these early hours

the hum of the 405 freeway

creeping through my window.

Sometimes I feel wonder

that I am able to wake up

other times the clarity is alarming

my thoughts refreshed by sleep

leading down tangential paths.

The belief that rising early brings reward

has a long history

from Confucius to Ben Franklin to the Dalai Lama–

It stems from our agrarian history

when we needed the daylight hours

to till the soil

to feed ourselves and family.

And even though I no longer farm the land
there is still magic left in these early hours.

50 YEARS PLUS 1 (REFLECTIONS ON THE END OF A DECADE)

1959 was quite a year.

I was seven years old.

My parents filmed my birthday party with a hand-held Kodak 16mm camera they had bought for $65.00. Because I got to watch it over and over again, it has become one of my earliest memories.

The world was new, and still growing, still full of discovery.

Westerns and Rod Serling were on the TV.

Hawaii and Alaska became our 49th and 50th states.

Doris Day and Frank Sinatra topped the pop charts.

Disney released "Sleeping Beauty", Alfred Hitchcock directed "North by Northwest" with Cary Grant, and Billy Wilder unleashed "Some Like It Hot" starring Marilyn Monroe, Jack Lemmon and Tony Curtis in drag.

It was a year that, looking back, many people say was the golden age of modern jazz. We saw the release of

-*Kind of Blue* by Miles Davis

-*Giant Steps* by John Coltrane

-*Take Five* by Dave Brubeck

Fifty years from now

our children, or our children's children will look back at the end of this past decade

(the oughts? The naughts? The "00's"? Maybe the ought nots?)

What will they see? What will they remember?

And can I live that legacy today,

a life worth living

a life worth remembering

a life worthy of greatness?

SELF-ESTEEM

Character is made up of many parts and can be seen many ways.

This is how other people see you,

and more important it is how you see yourself.

This self-esteem colors your days and activities.

There is a fine line between affirmation and delusion.

Sometimes I need to cross that line

and start from the belief that

self-esteem + action = accomplishment.

If the affirmation feels too big, it is probably kicking my self-esteem in the ass.

And it is okay to feel uncomfortable.

And it is okay to say

I have the talent

I have the ability

I have the time

I have the money

I have the desire

nothing can stop me now.

PURPOSEFUL ACTION

Ready, Fire, Aim!
is the way life often goes
but action without purpose
only works in the movies,
and only for so long.

Like climbing a mountain,
daily purposeful action
can achieve most any goal,
and the more I know the motivation
behind my action,
the more purposeful I become,
the more steps I will take
to reach the summit.

UP YOUR GAME

There are days when

all the preparation comes together,

you are at the top of your game

and then you surround yourself with the best

and it kicks your game up a notch.

The other night I got to play big

in celebration of my birthday.

I surrounded myself with great musicians

and played full out.

My game is about practice

about preparation

about giving

about sharing my passion

about inspiring others

about freedom

about heart.

Next time, if you want to play

I hope you can join me.

ACCOUNTABILITY

Setting a goal is great

Making a plan is also great

But who makes sure it gets done?

Who will keep you accountable?

This is possibly the trickiest challenge.

Left to my own devices

The entropy of the world takes over

I exercise less

I sleep a little more

I watch more TV

And I still get by.

"Getting by" is not what I want.

My passion lives in playing big

And to play big I must be accountable

To a partner

To a group

To a mentor

To myself.

The more accountability I have, the more likely I am to either complete the goal, or to admit

It is something I really don't want to do, and move on.

This is why sharing your goal is so important–

It is the first step towards accountability.

INSPECT WHAT YOU EXPECT

So you have a vision

of where you want to be a year from now.

And you have a goal

to help you get there.

What do you expect to happen when your vision is reality?

What do you expect to run into along the way?

Expectations can be too lofty or unreal,

you can reach your goal and be disappointed

or you can be unprepared for the success that follows.

How will this process affect your family?

How will it affect your friends?

How will it affect you?

So much of life is unknown and unpredictable

but if I inspect what I expect

there will be more purposeful action

and the results will be

achievable

realistic

more from my heart

less from my ego.

LIFE PURPOSE MAD LIBS

This whole purpose–mission–vision–goal thing is quite confusing.

If you have ever been to a planning retreat you know what I mean.

Spending hours sorting through the difference between how these four items relate to your business — or your life — is almost as much fun as a visit to the dentist.

It is pretty easy to set a goal, so why not just leave well enough alone?

Is this navel-gazing really worth the time?

It helps to think of your purpose as the view from 40,000 feet.

It's the bigger perspective

And now and then I need that sense of clarity.

Your purpose and your goal are two very different things.

Your goal may be to become a TV screenwriter,

but your purpose in life is not to be a TV screenwriter.

Your goal may be to make more money

but your purpose in life is not to make money.

The more your life is aligned with your purpose

the more joyful and passionate your life becomes.

Four years ago I discovered this simple formula to help find my purpose. This "Life Purpose Exercise" was created by Arnold M. Patent and it goes like this:

1) List two of your primary personal qualities, such as "enthusiasm" and "persistence". If you are not sure, ask someone who knows you well.

2) List one or two ways you enjoy expressing these qualities when interacting with others, such as "to support" and "to care for".

3) Assume the world is perfect right now. What does the world look like? How is everyone interacting with everyone else? What does it feel like? Write your answer in the present tense describing the perfect world as you see it and feel it. Remember, a perfect world is fun place to be.

Example: "Everyone is expressing their own unique talents. Everyone is working in harmony."

4) Now combine these items into a single statement:

My purpose is to use my _____(1)_____ and _____(1)_____ to _____(2)_____ and _____(2)_____ others to _____(3)_____.

A while ago I did this exercise.

Here were my answers:

1) Creativity, organization

2) To help, to inspire

3) There is enough for everyone. We are all working together to build better lives. Everyone works from a place of love.

And here is my life purpose:

"My purpose is to use my creativity and organization skills to inspire and help others to build a better life in abundance and love."

I had not looked back at this exercise for the last four years.

So, surprise

The pursuit of passion fits my life purpose.

WHAT DO YOU LOVE?

Sometimes we get so stuck in our heads

that we forget our hearts

we forget the purpose of all our getting.

At times like this it helps me

to stop

and make a list of everything that I love, everyone that I love

just a quick list, that starts every line with "I love..."

and give thanks for the ability

to know this

and to be able to choose from this list

and love today.

THE MOUNTAIN

Climbing the mountain

begins with a thought.

"I can do this."

Then a single step

starts me on my way.

The action

puts the thought to rest

and then once I am halfway through the journey

I have no choice but to continue.

Sending a rescue party

or a helicopter is not an option.

Whether it is putting $100 a month into savings

or producing a music album

or building a business

or mastering an instrument

or winning a gold medal in the Olympics

or hiking the Pacific Crest Trail.

It all begins with a thought

"I can do this"

and then a single step.

ATTACK LIFE WITH ENTHUSIASM

I had the strangest experience the other day.

I was in my local supermarket and went up to the Starbucks counter for a cup of coffee. Two very young people were behind the counter — they looked like they might just be out of high school.

"Hi, how ya doin' today?"

I got a very cheerful greeting.

"Fine, I'd like a tall coffee, and can I have your 'bold' blend?"

"Bold! You want 'bold' coffee?" one exclaimed, as the other went to fetch my drink. "Man, you must have a great day planned, that you need 'BOLD' coffee to get going!"

"Actually, this will be my third cup today..."

"Third cup! Man, you must be flying. You are sure going to have some day today!"

Never had I received so much enthusiasm with my cup of coffee.

And I thought, "This is weird."

But then I thought, imagine if the gal at the cleaners and the bank teller and the receptionist in my office all had this much enthusiasm.

So today, my friend, I will

attack life with enthusiasm

and see what happens.

THE WEEK THAT WILL BE

We stumble headlong into another day

our list of things to do growing,

items backing up like cars at a tollbooth

waiting to be charged and released.

But wait

the list has been grabbed by a bird

singing at sunrise

already in flight

announcing that this is not the week that was

this is the week that will be.

THE DANCE OF LIFE

I once saw the Merce Cunningham Dance Company

perform "Roaratorium", an hour-long work

inspired by James Joyce's "Finnegan's Wake"

with a sound collage by John Cage.

It was an hour of pure movement

structured, yet not totally prearranged

the disconnect between the movement and the music

unnerving at times,

and so surprising when the dance steps and the Irish music

fused.

There was a joy, a freedom,

created out of practice and training

beautiful to watch

astounding in its coming together,

the solo dances, the pas de deux, the ensemble movements

The journey lasted until the music ran out

until the dancers moved the stools from one side of the stage

to the other–

It is this journey, between what you once were

and what you are becoming–

this is where the dance of life takes place.

THE MUSE IN MUSIC

Although in Greek mythology there are nine muses, according to Pausanias (a Greek author and architect in the later second century A.D.), there were three original muses: Aoide ("song" or "voice"), Melete ("practice" or "occasion"), and Mneme ("memory").

These three elements are the foundation of music,

the purest art

and the least easy to value.

Music exists only in space,

in the distance between two points in time–

you cannot frame it

or admire it on a pedestal.

Perhaps this is my muse-

to share with others

for an evening or a day

my voice, my practice, my memory–

the joy of music making.

To give that generous gift

and then it is gone.

A DREAM

I carry the dream

of a small boy

wishing to create his own rules

create his own country,

where people live in peace and harmony

where creativity is the fuel,

where people love and respect art and music

and joy is the currency.

GIVE WHAT YOU CAN — WITH PASSION

*"We make a living with what we get, but we make a life
with what we give." –Winston Churchill*

As we move through life

from survival to significance

a dramatic change takes place

in what we give.

When I was young I thought that I had to build wealth before I

could give.

Then I realized that money was not a prerequisite–

I could do service, and give my time to things I cared about.

Giving time can be the greatest gift

it actually doesn't matter what, or how much you give.

If you give what you can, with passion

you can change the world.

CREATIVITY

I love being creative

in my work and my play.

The spark of creativity

is attractive.

We can do what is put in front of us

or we can create something

from what is given to us.

We can follow the recipe

or we can experiment by adding ingredients.

It can be as simple as,

instead of reading the rule book, asking:

"How can this be accomplished?"

and being open to the answer.

MOMENTUM

When you find what you are passionate about

what you love to do

what you are good at

the universe gives you momentum

to support the decision.

Like rolling down a hill

or floating on a river

once you get it going in the right direction

it becomes easier to grow,

to add more, to get bigger.

The momentum carries you further

than you thought possible.

When this happens it is time to ride the wave

avoiding obstacles that can affect your momentum.

I just need to get out of my own way.

WALK THROUGH FIRE

My greatest triumphs are not easy:

they take timing, strategy,

strength and commitment.

They often take me to dangerous places

way out of my comfort zone.

It could be a controlled burn in the forest or hot sand that can

burn my feet.

What do I have to lose? What do I have to gain?

To reach this level of greatness

the only way out is through

the house is on fire, and there's no turning back.

Sometimes getting to the finish line means

you have to walk through fire.

It is time to face my fears

and reach for the blaze of greatness,

reach for my highest self.

COMPETENCE—EXCELLENCE—BRILLIANCE

They say that practice makes perfect

I say practice makes you competent.

There are thousands of young violinists in the world

that have the facility to play the instrument

but lack the musicality

to get from competence to excellence.

In jazz it is the difference between knowing all the scales,

the licks and the chord substitutions

and just having those elements internalized to the point

where you no longer have to think about it — the music just

flows.

I want to be

more than competent

more than excellent

I want to find

that place in me where I shine

where intellect, talent and quality intersect

where the result is one of exultation

of creativity

of conspicuous talent

where I bring every aspect of myself together

and the result is brilliance.

LOVE THE PROCESS

Sometimes it feels so overwhelming

between job and life

practice, study and daily chores,

like a heavy weight

on my shoulders,

or like Sisyphus,

at the gym

on the StairMaster

climbing and climbing

but when you get off

you are in the same place that you started...

But life is not a curse,

it is a blessing

and this busyness

is self-imposed,

a desire to be all I am capable of being.

No one is telling me to live life at this pace

and I do it

because I love life and want to live it with passion.

This feeling of overwhelm turns around

when I love the process

and let go of the result.

LAUNCHING PAD

The ground must be level

and cleared of distractions

The time must be right

and the weather agreeable

to reach the destination.

Calculations are necessary

but must be flexible

due to constant change

in many variables.

The weeds must be removed

the flowers watered

the fire ignited

the combustion controlled

the excitement contained–

until that glorious moment

of lift-off.

And then

watching

the trajectory set

a happy landing

is almost guaranteed.

LIFE IS SHORT

What makes your heart race?

What makes your soul sing?

There is no more

"Maybe next year."

Set aside

The but and what if...

Life is short

Now's the time.

THE BEST THING

The best thing I can do today

is get up an hour early

and spend time with my dreams.

FEAR OF FLYING

Even if we don't know our Greek mythology,

we all know the lesson of Icarus.

Icarus put on wings and dared to fly.

Not only that, he dared to fly higher than anyone else.

The gods got angry at his daring

and the penalty was death.

We spend so much of our lives

being trained to fit in

to follow the rules

to stay in line.

We are taught not to stand up

or to stand out

or too fly too high

lest we anger the gods.

But what if

you were born to fly?

What if

you see something that needs to be done

and you have the will to do it?

What if

God smiles on your essential being

and does not see it as pride or arrogance

that you want to fly?

FEAR OF FLYING (PART 2)

Icarus received his wings from his father.

Everyone remembers his father's warning about flying

too close to the sun–

You might get burned, like the moth attracted to a flame.

But people forget his father's second warning, about

flying too close to the water, where the waves might affect

the lift of the wings–

You might drown by flying too low

just as easily as falling from the sky if you fly too high.

We follow our fear of flying too high

With the willingness to fly too low

Staying too safe

And in the end

Settling for too little.

The middle path

is not one of reckless stupidity

or mindless compliance.

It is one of being willing to risk,

flying higher than you ever thought imaginable

on the shoulders of our fathers

in a world where every day

the impossible

becomes possible.

WHAT IF IT WORKS?

Very often

when we get the big idea

the thought that stops us is

"What if I fail?"

But there are actually two kinds of afraid:

afraid of things that might fail

and afraid of things that might work.

I think my fear is

fear of failure,

but I know failure. I have experienced it

and know what it feels like.

The bigger unknown is usually

"What if I succeed?"

What if my big idea works,

thus changing everything

opening up a new set of

problems, relationships and fears?

The unknown is scary

will I be ready

when this big unknown called success

knocks on my door?

ACTUALIZING INSPIRATION FORMULA

We all have dreams and aspirations

but for many of us they remain just that–

a far-off idea

that turns into a "what if"

or "I could have" or "should have."

The trick is to grab that inspiration,

create a structure for it

and then commit to another person

that you will do what it takes

to make it happen.

It's a simple formula:

$$A = I \times (S + C)$$

Actualization = Inspiration x (Structure + Commitment)

FULL-HEARTEDNESS

I know I am in the right place

when I play with a full heart.

This full-heartedness

leads me to unusual places

where giving is common

and sharing joy is contagious.

Whether I am with 6,000 people

or two people

the spirit is the same.

Trusting my heart

listening to my heart

the doubts recede

and decisions are easy.

HONING YOUR VISION

Just as a craftsman needs to work with the most effective tools
I need to sharpen my vision every day.

Writing it out
reading it every week
sharing it with those I love.

Making it sharper
more efficient
more focused
the thought becomes reality.

And the more complete the picture
the more I see where I want to go
the clearer the path becomes.

BE MORE HUMAN

On my first recording date I had the honor of working

with the great jazz drummer, Billy Higgins.

We were sitting in the control room, listening back

to one of the tracks we had just finished.

It sounded great: note-perfect, vibrant, alive.

Then the engineer said,

"You know, the tempo sped up. The song ends

faster than it began."

And Billy said,

"So what? What do you think we are — machines?"

We are not machines

and the more we standardize

and follow instructions

the less human we become.

It is about the interaction between people

The call and response, the chance to riff and improvise

Without worrying about being perfect.

Feel is more important than tempo.

When I do this I become more human

more connected

more flexible

more resilient

more passionate.

THE POWER OF GRATITUDE

I used to think

asking for help was weakness

and showing thanks was weaker still,

admitting a second time

that I cannot do this alone.

But now I see

the power of gratitude.

It colors my sky

infusing my life with

joy and camaraderie.

I wake up in the morning

thankful that my feet touch the floor;

another day on this Earth

that the sun will kiss my skin,

my eyes will view dawn's arrival.

It is true

I cannot do this alone

and gratitude

is the cornerstone of abundance.

PASSION AND SKILL

You can be a skillful craftsman

but without passion for what you do

it is just a product.

You can be passionate about something

but without the skill to do it

the passion will fade to a hobby.

Great careers are found

at the intersection of passion and skill.

INSPIRATION IS OVERRATED

I love it when I feel inspired:

the spark of creativity

the great idea

the light bulb going off

the apple hitting my head

while I nap under the tree.

Life is 10% inspiration

and 90% perspiration.

The greatness is not in the idea

but in the execution of the idea.

It is easy to keep napping,

even after the apple bonks you on the head.

The real challenge in life

is carrying the inspiration

into the mundane everyday

and making the thought into reality.

A SENSE OF ADVENTURE

Each day as I awaken

and my feet hit the floor

I realize that it is another day in the adventure travel business:

- There are copious amounts of moving parts that have to be coordinated.

- As the leader, you have to be an expert in the area you are traveling in.

- Timing and positioning is everything.

- You have to be flexible and open to change.

- There's always something new around every corner.

- The itinerary might say we are going to fly, but be ready to get on a boat instead.

- You plan for the best, but prepare for the worst.

- Before the trip is done, you are bound to experience something you never thought would happen.

- There may be turbulence, but as long as you stay in your seat, you will get to the destination. Just don't jump up and start trying to fly the plane yourself.

- And bring your sense of adventure!

OBSTACLES

Sometimes I forget why I am here

the daily grind gets too difficult

the road too steep

the obstacles too huge.

It reminds me of an inner-city elementary school class

on its first trip to a national forest.

Just imagine

children that have never been in the woods

hiking on a well-marked dirt trail

and they come to a large tree,

fallen across the path.

The children yell,

"Our path is blocked! We have to turn back!"

It is only with the teacher's encouragement

the children realize

they can leave the path and walk around the tree,

perhaps even climb on top of it

for a better view

of things to come.

ANNIVERSARY

It is quite coincidental

that I began my Passion Party on May 26, 2009,

the same day as my wedding anniversary.

So now each year I get to celebrate two anniversaries:

the anniversary of my marriage to Diana,

the light of my life,

and the anniversary of my morning ritual

and the Passion Party.

For me it has been a year of growth,

of acknowledgment, of meditation,

of restructuring my business

for a new world with new rules

coming from a place of anger, frustration and pity

to a place of possibility, love and passion.

MY WISH

My wish for you

is that when you turn 90

you can look back and say,

"All in all,

things have turned out pretty good."

ACKNOWLEDGMENTS

I want to thank, with gratitude, some of the people that made this book possible:

- Joe Stumpf, my business coach for the last 14 years, who continues to inspire me and prod me forward. He was the instigator that started this writing adventure, and has been there for mental and spiritual support throughout. Joe, without you I am sure this book would still be stuck somewhere "in process". http://www.byreferralonly.com

- My wife, Diana – Without your support and understanding I could not possibly do what I do. I love you.

- My sons, Benjamin and Evan – On a subconscious level, the motivation to write this book has been to share with you thoughts and wisdom that I felt uncomfortable speaking directly to you both. You inspire me to share the best I can be.

- Dr. Michael Murphy – The editor of the *Pursuit of Passion* poems. Thank you for your knowledge and guidance.

- C. Spencer Reynolds – My go-to guy to take the project across the finish line and make the layout look beautiful in print and digital. http://SpencerReynolds.com

- Kurt Michelson – For the fantastic cover of the book. A very gifted graphic artist. http://dribbble.com/thewordkurt

- Mara Zaslove – For the wonderful photo on the back cover.

Evan Kahn – The perfect person to do the final copy editing. All those years on the college newspaper are starting to pay off!

I would also like to thank people that inspired some of the writing in this book:

Seth Godin   http://www.sethgodin.com/sg

Jack Canfield   http://jackcanfield.com

Malcolm Gladwell   http://www.gladwell.com

Arnold M. Patent   http://www.arnoldpatent.com/wordpress

ABOUT THE ARTWORK

At a very young age I became interested in puzzles and mazes.

Making my own designs and mazes was much more fun than trying to solve mazes in a book. I spent many hours during boring days in middle school and high school, doodling mazes on graph paper (as well as in the history textbook, which got me into trouble).

My friends and I would trade these mazes, trying to stump each other. We made mazes that included bridges, or even holes in the paper that would make you fall through to the other side, where the maze would continue.

When I finally moved on to college, I kept one folder filled with these mazes, thinking that someday they might be fun to play with.

Then life happened. Years passed.

There were twists and turns, places where I fell through the floor and felt like I would not find my way out—many years where, looking forward, I could not really see the path I was on. I just knew that I was still putting one foot in front of the other.

A recent college reunion found me digging around in the garage, and I came upon a box marked "High School 1969".

I started looking through this old box of photos and writings and, lo and behold, I came upon my "puzzle and maze" folder. And then it occurred to me that the maze was a great visual for the process of finding one's passion, finding the way to navigate through the world to find one's own heart, and the heart's desire.

A maze with the heart as the final destination.

These mazes were tough and convoluted, but then I remembered one of the secrets to solving a maze.

The fastest way to solve a maze is to start at the end and follow them backwards to the beginning.

This may be one of the secrets of life, as well as mazes:

> *If you start at the end, the path reveals itself, and the maze becomes easy.* —George Kahn

ABOUT THE AUTHOR

GEORGE KAHN has been called the "Money Man By Day, Jazzman By Night". In addition to being Senior Vice President of a successful mortgage bank, he is also an accomplished jazz pianist and composer, with seven albums released and an eighth album in the works. He performs often with his quintet at clubs in the Los Angeles area, and his music can be heard on jazz stations across the country, as well as in various movies and television shows.

Photo by Mara Zaslove

For more information about George's music, please visit

http://georgekahn.com

This is George's first book of collected writings from his Passion Party blog

http://pursuitofpassionbooks.com

http://passionparty09.blogspot.com

THE MUSIC OF GEORGE KAHN

Secrets From The Jazz Ghetto

...Compared To What?

Freedom Vessel

Conscious Dreams

Cover Up!

Midnight Brew

Out of Time

All are available on iTunes

Made in the USA
Charleston, SC
07 December 2013